AMAZING ANIMAL HOMES

BELINDA WEBER

CONTENTS

Project Manager: Belinda Weber
Art Editor: Eljay Yildirim
DTP Manager: Nicky Studdart
Production Controller: Jo Blackmore

KINGFISHER/UNIVERSAL
Kingfisher Publications Plc
New Penderel House
283-288 High Holborn
London WC1V 7HZ
www.kingfisherpub.com

First published by Kingfisher Publications Plc 2002

10 9 8 7 6 5 4 3 2 1

1TR/1201/TWP/MAR(MAR)/130SINAR

A CIP catalogue record for this book is available from the British Library.

ISBN 0 7534 0736 1

Printed in Singapore

Woody Woodpecker™ needs a new home. The one he's got is too small and there are holes in the roof that let the rain in. He wants his new home to be a bit different so he's looking at his friends' homes to get some new ideas.

The one thing all his friends say is that his home should be safe. He needs to be sure that no uninvited guests can surprise him and that it will protect him from the weather.

Looking around him, Woody™ can see that animals have made their homes just about everywhere. Some live under the water, while others cling to the edges of cliffs. But all the homes offer some protection and a safe place to mate and raise a family.

Beside the sea

Some animals carry their homes with them, but Woody™ doesn't think this is such a good idea. Where would he keep all his bits and pieces? Limpets cling to seashore rocks and are battered by the waves. When the tide is out, limpets clamp their shells to the rocks. But when the tide comes in, they loosen their grip and wander over the rocks to feed.

Wacky World

When a razor shell feels threatened it quickly pulls itself into the sand. It is so fast, it can burrow down to half its shell length in just one second.

FEATHERY FINGERS

Sea anemones live in shallow seas and attach themselves to rocks or near the bottom of weeds.

LIVING STARS

Most starfish have five arms. The underside of each arm is covered with little suckers. Starfish move by fixing their suckers to rocks and pulling themselves forward.

4

Mobile homes

Hermit crabs have long, soft bodies, so need a home that will protect them. They find empty seashells and back into them. As the crab grows, it has to find a bigger shell to live in. Sea anemones sometimes live on the hermit crab's shell. They protect the crab with their stinging tentacles, and the crab carries them to new feeding grounds.

ALL CHANGE!
When a hermit crab moves to a larger shell, the crab prods and pokes at the sea anemones until they move to the new one.

WALKING ON THE SEABED
Prawns live close to the shore. Although they can swim, prawns prefer to walk along the sandy seabed in search of food. They are scavengers and eat any dead creatures they find.

Taking to the skies

Looking up, Woody™ spots some birds circling. "Where do they live?," he wonders. The cliffs may look uninviting, but Woody can see that lots of birds, including gulls, have made their homes here.

DIGGING IN THE TURF

Puffins make their homes by digging holes in the soft turf with their beaks. Some take over old rabbit burrows. They lay their eggs and raise their young in these holes. Puffins bring their young fish to eat. They can carry up to 12 fish at a time.

Sitting on seaweed

Gulls and some other seabirds nest on rocky islands or ledges. They make their nests from mud or seaweed and the females lay their eggs in them. Lots of birds nest beside each other, and noisy squabbles break out if they get too close.

FEATHER BEDS

Eider ducks find a hollow in the rocks in which to make their nests. They make it cosy by lining it with seaweed and soft feathers pulled from the female's breast.

Wacky World

American bald eagles fly back to the same nest every year. Some nests are over 100 years old and can be bigger than a car. The eagles repair the nests, then raise a new family.

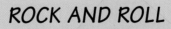

ROCK AND ROLL

Guillemots don't make nests. They lay pointed eggs straight on to a rocky ledge. If the egg is knocked, it will roll around in a circle on the pointy end and not fall off.

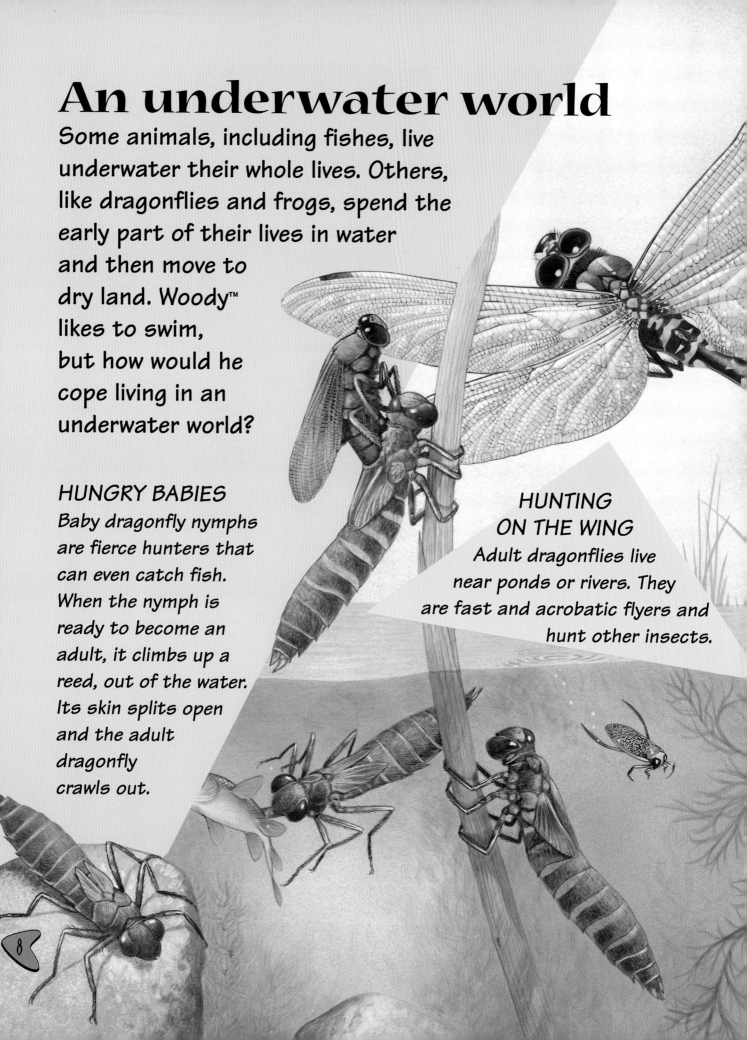

An underwater world

Some animals, including fishes, live underwater their whole lives. Others, like dragonflies and frogs, spend the early part of their lives in water and then move to dry land. Woody™ likes to swim, but how would he cope living in an underwater world?

HUNGRY BABIES

Baby dragonfly nymphs are fierce hunters that can even catch fish. When the nymph is ready to become an adult, it climbs up a reed, out of the water. Its skin splits open and the adult dragonfly crawls out.

HUNTING ON THE WING

Adult dragonflies live near ponds or rivers. They are fast and acrobatic flyers and hunt other insects.

8

Some spiders like to go fishing for their food. Swamp spiders paddle their feet in the water and wriggle them as bait for tiny fish. As soon as any fishes nibble at the spider's feet, it grabs them for a tasty snack.

DIVING FOR FISH

Diving beetles also make their homes underwater. They trap air under their wing cases so that they can breathe. Diving beetle larvae are called water tigers. They can catch fish.

CAMPING IN BUBBLES

Water spiders breathe air, but they live underwater. They spin basket-like webs, and hang them upside-down from water plants. The spider fills the web with bubbles of air from the surface.

Busy builders

Beavers cut down trees with their sharp teeth and use them to dam rivers and make small lakes. Beavers build their homes in the middle of these lakes, where they are safe from attack. Woody™ thinks it would be very hard to build a home like this!

STRONG TEETH
A beaver's teeth are so strong that they can cut down trees with trunks up to one metre across.

Living in tunnels

Moles are expert burrowers, digging tunnels deep underground in which to live. While Woody™ can see that this is a safe idea, he is not sure he would like living in a tunnel.

Speedy feet

Wombats dig burrows with their powerful front feet and impressive claws. The burrows can be up to 30 metres long. The wombats sleep in them during the day, coming out at night to feed.

UNDERWATER DOORS

All the entrances to the beavers' home are underwater, so other animals can't get in.

Wacky World

Beavers use their tails in many ways. When swimming, they use them for steering, and on land they rest on them while gnawing trees. If a beaver spots an enemy, it slaps its tail on the water. The sound warns other beavers of the danger.

Wasp worlds

Some animals build a huge home in which to live. Bees and wasps often live in large groups and work together to look after their homes. Paper wasps chew strips of wood into a paste that they spread in thin layers to build their nest. Woody™ doesn't think the walls would be strong enough for him!

MAKING CLAY CUPS

The female potter wasp makes little cups from mud and saliva to house her eggs. The wasp stings and paralyses a caterpillar and puts it inside the cup. She then lays an egg on top. When the young wasp hatches, it has plenty of fresh food to eat!

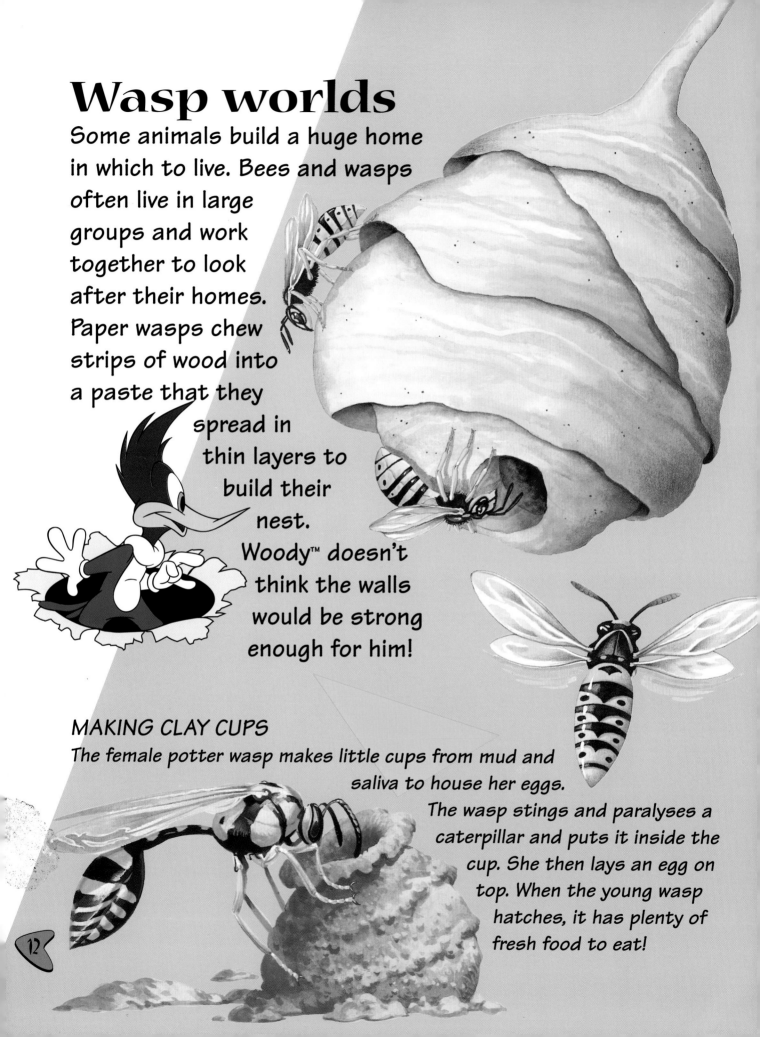

Living in a wax world

Honeybees make their nests in the hollows of trees or under branches. They make sheets of wax and build a honeycomb of six-sided cells. In some of the cells, the queen lays her eggs, which are looked after by the workers. In other cells, the worker bees store pollen, or honey, which they make from the sweet nectar of flowers.

FLY AWAY BEES

Bees swarm when their nests are too full. A new queen and some workers leave to make a new nest.

LIVING IN A HOLE!

Bumblebees build small nests underground, often in old mouse holes. The nest may be home to 100 bumblebees.

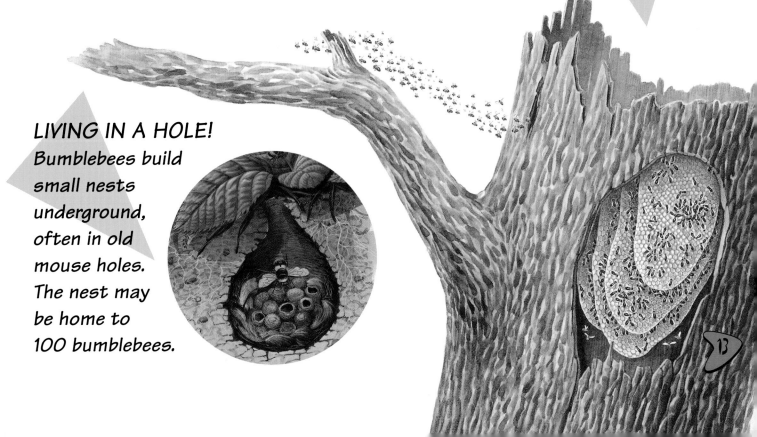

Building cities

Ants and termites live in huge colonies. One female, the queen, lays all the eggs. She is looked after by other members of the colony. Woody™ likes this idea, but doesn't think his friends will look after him!

Termite towns

Termites are the champion builders of the insect world. They mix their saliva with mud to make nests that can stand 12 metres high. In the breeding season, termites grow wings and some males and females fly away to start new nests.

STICKY LARVAE

Weaver ants make a nest from leaves that they stick together. They use their larvae, or young, as living tubes of glue. Each worker holds a larva in its jaws and moves it backwards and forwards between two leaves. The larva leaves a sticky, silky thread that glues the two leaves together.

GARDENING ANTS

Leafcutter ants live in nests with fungus gardens. The ants collect bits of leaves and take them to their gardens. The fungus grows on the leaves, and the ants then eat the fungus.

LIVING STORE CUPBOARDS

Honeypot ants live in underground nests. Some worker ants cling to the ceilings and become living storage jars. When there is a lot of food, they are filled with nectar. When there is less food, other workers 'milk' them for their nectar.

15

Boring homes

Birds do not live in nests all year round. They build them to protect their eggs and young. Some birds don't build their homes, but bore them out of trees. Woody™ knows all about this style of housing, but he wouldn't choose a spiky cactus to start from!

What, no trees?

The gila woodpecker can't find trees in its desert home. Instead it bores a hole in the tree-shaped, giant saguaro cactus. The flesh of the cactus dries out around the hole, making it a snug and cosy place to raise a family. Because of the sharp spines on the cactus, few enemies can reach the woodpeckers.

LOCKED IN?

The female hornbill walls herself inside a hole in a tree and lays her eggs. With only her bill sticking out of the tree, the male feeds her while she waits for her eggs to hatch.

MY TURN NOW!

When the gila woodpecker has finished with its nest, there are lots of other animals, including elf owls, keen to take over its safe home. Elf owls are the smallest owls in the world. They hunt at night and spend their days resting in their holes.

FEATHERED FUN!

What do you get if you cross a chicken with a cement mixer?

A brick layer!

FEATHERED FUN!

Why don't ducks tell jokes when they're flying?

In case they quack up!

Weavers and tailors

Some birds make very fancy nests to help them find a mate. Tailorbirds and weaverbirds hang their nests from trees, safe from most predators. Woody™ isn't sure if he'd have enough room in one of these homes, so he'll look for something larger.

DESIGNER HOMES

The male weaverbird has to make a perfect nest. If it doesn't look good enough, no female will mate with him. He hangs from a branch weaving long strips of grass into a hollow ball, in which the female will lay her eggs.

SKILFUL SEWING

The tailorbird is one of the most skilful nest builders in the world. Using its beak as a needle and spiders' silk as thread, it stitches leaves together to make a pouch. It lines the pouch with grass or hair and then the female lays her eggs inside.

BAKED HOMES

Ovenbirds use wet mud and straw to make their nests, which become rock-hard when they dry. They are shaped like old-fashioned clay ovens, and are built on branches or gate posts.

Wacky World

Swifts and swiftlets have large saliva glands that produce a gluey substance that holds their nests together. Cave swiftlets from Southeast Asia make their whole nests out of this saliva. Local people collect the nests and sell them to restaurants. They are served as 'birds' nest soup'.

COMPOST NESTS

The mallee fowl lays its eggs in a huge nest mound made of sand and fallen leaves. As the leaves rot, the temperature rises allowing the eggs to develop. The male mallee fowl checks the mound each day. If it is too hot, he opens it up a bit to cool down the eggs.

19

At home underground

Prairie dogs are ground-dwelling squirrels that live on the grassy plains of central USA. They dig a network of tunnels and burrows. Woody™ thinks the tunnels might be too crowded for him!

ON GUARD DUTY

During the day, some prairie dogs keep watch for enemies. If they are startled, they warn the others, and hurry back to the burrows.

Wacky World

Arctic ground squirrels living in northern Canada and Alaska hold the record for the longest hibernation of all the rodents. They sleep for nine months of each year. During the remaining three, they eat, breed and store food in their burrows.

Sleepy heads

In cold places, brown bears hibernate in winter. This means that they sleep very deeply for the cold months when food is short. Some bears dig dens underground, but others find caves and snuggle down for the winter. They sometimes share their home with other animals, including bats.

HIDDEN TREASURES

Dung beetles are so-called because they eat animal dung. They roll it into a ball and bury it underground. Females also bury balls of dung for their eggs. When the young beetles hatch, they have a supply of food waiting for them.

FEATHERED FUN!

How does a bear get down from a tree?

It sits on a leaf and waits 'til autumn.

21

In the trees

Chimpanzees are apes that live in large groups in grasslands and open woodlands in Africa. Chimps spend a lot of time in trees. At night, they build nests from leaves and sleep high above the ground. Woody™ likes tree houses, but wants a longer-lasting home.

BEING FRIENDLY

Chimpanzees live in small, sociable groups. They groom each other to remove small insects and dirt from their fur.

COLOURFUL CHATTERERS

Eclectus parrots make their nests in holes in trees. They are colourful and noisy birds, that shriek and chatter as they fly about searching for fruit and flower buds to eat.

NOISY HOWLERS

Howler monkeys are the noisiest creatures in the forests. Their voices can carry for about five kilometres. Groups of howlers live in the topmost branches of trees, eating leaves. They occasionally climb down to the ground.

Living in a coral world

Corals look like stones, but they are tiny animals that live together. Corals live in warm, shallow seas. Woody™ can't live underwater, but lots of other animals make their homes there.

FLOWER POWER

Sea anemones live on coral reefs. They look a bit like flowers, but are really animals. Sea anemones catch their food in their long, stinging tentacles.

SPECIAL SLIME

Clown fish can live in a sea anemone's stinging tentacles without any harm. Their bodies are protected by a special slime.

Wacky World

Crown-of-thorns starfish are big starfish that have as many as 19 arms. They eat the tiny corals, leaving just their hard skeletons behind.

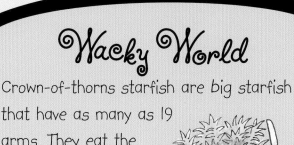

BATHING BEAUTIES

Sponges are very simple animals. They feed by sucking water in through small openings and filtering out any food.

NOISY EATERS

Parrotfish live on coral reefs. They even bite bits off to eat. Their loud crunching can be heard several metres away.

COLOURFUL SWIMMERS

Butterfly fish make their homes on coral reefs. They feed on different parts of the coral.

City life

Rats and many other animals find that people have moved in on their homes, leaving them nowhere to go. Woody™ knows that sometimes you just have to make the best of it, and live alongside people.

NEW HOMES IN THE CITY

Foxes are shy creatures that usually live in dens in woods or open grassland. Many now make their homes in gardens and even busy city centres.

NEIGHBOURHOOD WATCH!

Raccoons can make a home almost anywhere! Usually found in woodlands, raccoons have mastered the art of living in towns. In woods, they eat frogs and fruit, but in towns they raid rubbish bins for tasty scraps.

Wacky World

Raccoons are mischievous animals that have learnt to live alongside humans. They are intelligent and extremely good at using their paws. They can unscrew the lids from jars and take the stoppers out of bottles to get to the contents. They even break into tents and trailers at campsites.

THE HIGH LIFE

Storks sometimes make their nests on rooftops, close to open fields. They feed on small animals that they catch there.

FEATHERED FUN!

What do you get if you pour boiling water down a rabbit hole?

Hot cross bunnies!

FEATHERED FUN!

What do mice do in the daytime?

Mouse-work!

Living together

Sometimes animals, called parasites, make their homes on other animals! Woody™ knows how difficult it is to cope with uninvited guests when Knothead™ and Splinter™ come to visit, but these parasites can prove to be even more annoying! Some eat dead skin, while others, like fleas, bite the host animal and drink its blood.

YOU SCRATCH MY BACK...

Baboons and other monkeys spend a lot of time grooming each other. This mother is grooming her baby by parting its fur and picking out any insects or dirt. Fleas are parasites that live in the fur of other animals. Their bodies are very narrow so they can slip through the hairs or feathers. Their bites can leave itchy spots on the host animal.

28

FOOD ON THE MOVE

Oxpeckers find their food on the backs of rhinos and other grazing mammals. They scamper over these beasts picking off ticks and other parasites. If something startles the birds, they scuttle around the rhino until they are completely hidden.

Animals that live by themselves have to find a way to get rid of any itchy mites that live in their fur. Giant pandas like to roll in the dust. The gritty sand rubs off the mites, helping to keep the panda's skin and fur healthy and in good condition.

WHO LIVES WHERE?!!

1. WHO LIVES IN A STAR?
a) Hermit crab
b) Dung beetle
c) Starfish
d) Chimpanzee

2. WHO LIVES IN A BUBBLE OF AIR?
a) Eider duck
b) Howler monkey
c) Raccoon
d) Water spider

3. WHO LIVES IN AN EMPTY RABBIT BURROW?
a) Rhino
b) Puffin
c) Butterfly fish
d) Baboon

4. WHO WIGGLES ITS FEET WHEN FISHING FOR FOOD?
a) Swamp spider
b) Fox
c) Giant panda
d) Brown bear

5. WHO CUTS DOWN TREES TO MAKE ITS HOME?
a) Leafcutter ant
b) Eclectus parrot
c) Beaver
d) Diving beetle

6. WHO WALLS HERSELF INSIDE A TREE WITH HER EGGS?

a) Hornbill

b) Prairie dog

c) Weaver ant

d) Mallee fowl

7. WHO MAKES ITS NEST IN A MOUND OF ROTTING LEAVES?

a) Mallee fowl

b) Guillemot

c) Sea anemone

d) Wombat

8. WHICH ANIMAL MAKES ITS NEST FROM PAPER?

a) Elf owl

b) Paper wasp

c) Clown fish

d) Stork

9. WHICH ANIMAL MAKES A NEST IN THE BRANCHES EVERY NIGHT?

a) Chimpanzee

b) Rhino

c) Beaver

d) Raccoon

10. WHICH BIRD FLIES BACK TO THE SAME NEST EVERY YEAR?

a) American bald eagle

b) Guillemot

c) Tailorbird

d) Parrotfish

Answers

1. c; 2. d; 3. b; 4. a; 5. c; 6. a; 7. a; 8. b; 9. a; 10. a.

Index